RUMI

Know that it is the waves of love which turn the wheels of heaven;
without love the world would be without life.

In December of each year, in the town of Konya in Turkey, the death of the great religious poet, Jalaluddin Rumi, is celebrated with music and the special dancing for which his followers, known as the "Whirling Dervishes", are famous. It was in Konya in December of 1273 that Rumi died and it was there that he composed his great book of poetry, the Mathnavi.

Even as a young boy, Rumi's exceptional abilities were recognised. The story is told of how his father took him on a visit to the Persian poet, Attar, author of the famous long poem "The

Conference of the Birds." The elderly Attar was so impressed by the boy that he presented him with one of his books.

Another story tells that, at the age of eleven, Rumi was playing on the flat roof of his parents' house with some of his young friends. The other children then suggested that they should continue their games in the house next door. Rumi said that he preferred to go directly to the opposite roof rather than go down the stairs in his own house and up the stairs in the neighbouring one. But the two houses were divided by a large gap and Rumi's friends made fun of him: how could he possibly jump across such a wide space? However, having left him on his own, his friends were amazed to find Rumi already waiting for them on the roof of the other house. How did he do it, they wondered.

Rumi was born in the city of Balkh in the country which is known today as Afghanistan. His father was a famous man of religion and a great scholar, and was descended from the first Caliph of Islam, Abu Bakr. Thus Rumi grew up in an atmosphere of learning and strict Islamic teaching. When he was still a young boy, the family moved from Balkh, which was then being threatened by the Mongols, a warlike people from the East. In

RUMI
POET AND SAGE

by
DENYS JOHNSON-DAVIES
&
Illustrated by
LAURA DE LA MARE

HOOD HOOD BOOKS

Hood Hood Books
46 Clabon Mews
London SW1X OEH
Tel: 44.171. 5847878
Fax: 44.171. 2250386

British Library Cataloguing–in–Publication Data
A catalogue record for this book is available from the British Library

ISBN 1 900251 04 3

Origination: Fine Line Graphics-London
Printed by IPH, Egypt

3

fact, two years later, Balkh was destroyed by the Mongols and thousands of people were murdered.

On leaving Balkh, Rumi's father took his family on the pilgrimage to Mecca, and later lived for a while in Damascus and Aleppo before settling in the town of Konya in present-day Turkey. Konya was the ideal place in which to set up a new home, for at that time it seemed as far away as possible from attack by the Mongols; also it was a place to which a number of scholars from all over the Islamic world had come.

Rumi's father quickly made himself a reputation as a teacher in Konya. By this time his son had grown up and was married, and was himself recognised for his great learning.

Politically, these were troubled years and only too soon the Mongol armies had moved further on in their conquests and were threatening the town of Konya. It was in this period that Rumi experienced the most important event in his life, an event that was to change him dramatically. In the year 1244 he met a certain Shamsuddin Tabrizi, a man who had given up normal life and become a wandering Sufi or dervish. Sufis are Muslim men and women who give up normal life and devote themselves to trying

to understand the great mystery of God.

This man, Shamsuddin (his name in Arabic means "Sun of Religion"), was a strange and unusual man who had wandered through much of the Muslim world in search of someone from whom he could gain knowledge of life's mysteries. Shamsuddin had none of the worldly ambitions for fine clothes or good food, for money or social position: he also cared nothing for the opinions of his fellow men and he could be blunt, even rude. He was some ten years older than Rumi. They first met in Konya in a caravanserai, an inn where penniless travellers were able to stay.

Rumi saw in Shamsuddin a man who, unlike anyone else he had met, had the courage to reject all those things for which most people strive: security, fame and money. Immediately, he began to spend most of the hours of the day and night in conversation with Shamsuddin. Soon Rumi gave up visiting the high-class society of sheikhs, scholars and men of letters, of which he had been a respected member, and became, like his friend, a person uninterested in worldly matters.

It was natural that Rumi's former friends, with whom he no longer associated, should feel jealous of this stranger to whom

Rumi now gave all his time and attention. Rumi's second son was especially bitter about this stranger who had entered the family house and become his father's closest friend. Shamsuddin, on his side, became aware that his presence in Konya and his influence over Rumi, were resented by many people. Whatever the reason – perhaps his life was threatened by his enemies – Shamsuddin suddenly decided to leave Konya.

But, had Shamsuddin really just left the house and gone away? According to a writer of the time, while Rumi and Shamsuddin were once talking deep into the night, there came a knock at the door and Shamsuddin was called outside. For an hour Rumi waited for his friend, but then, becoming suspicious, he himself stepped into the night and called out his name. There was no answer. Alarmed, Rumi looked around the garden but to no avail. It was dark and difficult to see anything, so all he could do was go back inside and wait until dawn when he could resume his search. It was only then, however, that he discovered the horror of what had taken place. Shamsuddin had been set upon by a man who had stabbed him to death and thrown his body down a well. This brutal murder was apparently arranged by Rumi's

second son.

Rumi continued to lead a life devoted to prayer and fasting, teaching his followers and helping those less fortunate than himself. He never asked for anything for himself but would often seek the assistance of the rich and powerful in Konya on behalf of others. He would be pleased when he found there was nothing to eat in his house and would remark: "Today our house is like those of the saints."

He would spend much of his time in meditation, for he trained himself to sleep little and to eat only as much as his body required. One of his simple pleasures was to go outside the town on a summer's day to picnic with his friends and followers, and to enjoy the peace of the countryside and the gentle sound of the turning of the watermill.

It was at this time that Rumi made a close friend of a man by the name of Chalabi. This man was a merchant in Konya and had known Rumi for many years. It was Chalabi who was able to persuade Rumi that he should write down his teachings in a book for the benefit of his many followers, and for future generations. Up until that time, Rumi's disciples had been studying the

writings of other Persian poets. Rumi now dictated to his friend Chalabi the enormous masterpiece which has become known as the Mathnavi. This is a book of poetry which consists of no less than six volumes containing nearly 30,000 verses. Chalabi would write down all the verses that Rumi dictated – either when they were sitting together in his house, or walking along the street, or wherever they happened to be. The verses would then be read over and, if necessary, corrected. Today the Mathnavi is read all over the world, both in the original Persian and in the many translations that have been made of it. It has become one of the most important books of poetry.

In 1273 Rumi became ill and the doctors were unable to find out what was wrong. Gradually he became weaker and soon it was clear that he would not recover. From all around people came to call on him and pay their respects. While on his death-bed he consoled his visitors by reciting poems about Paradise and the Angels.

In one of his most famous stories, Rumi shows how death cannot be avoided. One day the Prophet, King Solomon, was sitting on his throne when a man called Ali came to see him, his face white with terror.

"What is the matter?" enquired Solomon.

"Your Majesty," the man stuttered, "I have just seen the Angel of Death, and he was looking at me in a very peculiar way. He was frowning. Your Majesty, you must help me!"

"But what can I do?"

"Command the winds to transport me to ... to ... Hindustan! Perhaps there I can seek refuge."

Solomon sighed, for he knew that the Angel of Death appearing to Ali meant that his time on earth had come to an end. There was no place for him to hide. Nevertheless, Ali was a friend of his, so he commanded the winds to transport him thousands of miles away, which they did in the blink of an eye.

Later that evening, Solomon summoned the Angel of Death. "Tell me," he asked, "why were you looking at our friend, Ali, in such a peculiar way?"

"Your Majesty (it must not be forgotten that Prophets are

closer to God than angels), I was told yesterday morning that this man's time on earth had come to an end in Hindustan, and that I was instructed to transport his soul Heavenwards. Imagine my surprise when, visiting your court this morning to pay my respects, I saw the very man standing in your presence. My peculiar expression was down to my confusion. For how could this man, whose soul I was to take in Hindustan, be standing in this court? Anyway, to cut a long story short, I've just returned from there and you will be relieved to hear that Ali is safe in Heaven."

Solomon reflected to himself that no power on earth, not even those of Prophets, could deflect man from his destiny, or from his death; he knew that God's will could not be avoided.

The Mathnavi and Rumi's other writings contain numerous stories that are full of delightful wisdom. Many of them are about animals, because, like other great Islamic thinkers, he had read the stories in the classical work, "Kalila wa Dimna," where

animals are used to illustrate truths about life. Thus Rumi says:

"Let us, for instance, suppose you put a gold collar on a dog. You will not consider it to be a hunting dog just because you have put a gold collar around its neck. A hunting dog has a particular quality, whether it has a collar of gold or a piece of string around its neck. So, in the same way, a man does not become a scholar by reason of wearing a fine gown and a turban."

Almost every animal and bird has its place in Rumi's great poem. The camel, the main means of transport in those times in that part of the world, is of course there, listening to the voice of its rider as he encourages it with his singing. Dogs and cats are to be found as the central characters in a number of stories. In one, the cat is described as the policeman who, if it keeps awake and does not neglect its duty, keeps the house free from mice. The dog is sometimes held up as an example to men. Rumi points out that the dog is not content to lie back and sleep, hoping that someone will give it something to eat. The dog asks for food and wags its tail, while most men do nothing about asking of God the good things that He is able to give. "So why do you not wag your tail?" Rumi asks of men.

Rumi uses lions and foxes, jackals and donkeys, to illustrate certain situations in which man finds himself. He also employs the smallest and most insignificant of creatures, such as bees and ants (both have chapters in the Quran named after them) to show how clever and industrious they are.

Rumi also writes about the different kinds of birds. The nightingale, with its beautiful voice, the parrot with its ability to imitate human speech, the falcon that man traps and trains to hunt for him, the peacock which is the symbol of pride and arrogance. Then there is the rooster which is praised because it calls men and women to prayer in the early morning.

There is a story about Rumi wanting to meditate near a pond, but the frogs disturb him with their croaking: "When you can say something better", he tells them, "then talk – otherwise listen." And the frogs fell silent.

Although Rumi's tales of animals are very entertaining, they always convey a deeper message. One day a lion-cub went out

wandering alone until he found himself lost. He looked around frantically but there was no sign of his parents or of any other lions who could point him in the right direction. Being by nature a lion, he did not feel afraid and he lay down in the afternoon sun and fell asleep. On waking up, the cub rubbed his eyes only to see himself surrounded by a flock of sheep.

"Baa!" they greeted him. And since the cub was still too young to understand that he was a lion, he thought he was a sheep.

"Baa!" he returned their greeting, and began to play and frolic with them.

The days passed and the sheep-cub remained with the flock. He would bounce and frolic and play with them, though he could not understand a word they were saying, apart from Baa! that is. He realised that he could run faster than they could, see further, and hear better. He was also *always* hungry. Eating grass was amusing, but there was nothing like a piece of meat!

Sometimes a sound in the distance would make the sheep run off in panic while he would hardly flinch. One morning, while the sheep were grazing, a sound was heard in the nearby thicket.

They pricked up their ears and, before the cub could even blink, the sheep were all fleeing in terror. Approaching the flock was a lion. How silly, the cub thought to himself, who would be scared of a lion?

"Baa!" he said, bouncing up to the lion.

"ROAR!" The poor cub was thrown back by the ferocity of the lion's roar.

"Come with me," commanded the lion, and he marched along while the cub bounced. Shortly afterwards they reached a lake.

"Look in the water," he ordered the cub, who crept to the edge and glanced in. "You are a lion, son of a lion, grandson of a lion. Not a sheep. Now roar with me. ROAR!"

"Baa!"

"ROAR!"

"Braar!"

"ROAR!"

"Roar!"

"That is better."

And, you know, it was much better. The sheep-cub felt the energy flowing back in him. Baaing was fine for what it was but

there was nothing like a good roar. He now understood that he wasn't a sheep-cub but a lion-cub!

"Now I will take you back to your parents. And do not forget who you are. A lion is the king of animals. Just because some sheep baa at you does not mean that you forget who you are."

In this way, Rumi uses the story of the lion-cub who thought he was a sheep, to show how man can only be happy when he is true to himself.

Rumi was particularly fond of cats. It is related that, at his death, his cat refused to eat any food and died a week later. Rumi's daughter buried the cat close to her father's tomb.

At sunset on December 17th 1273, Rumi died. Many people were at his burial, not only Muslims but also Jews and Christians, for Rumi had always shown himself to be understanding of other religions. Today, more than seven hundred years after his death, people still make the journey to Konya to visit the tomb of Rumi, one of the world's greatest poets and sages.

21

HEROES FROM THE EAST

· SALADIN ·

MARION KHALIDI

· SINAN ·

EMMA CLARK

· QUEEN OF SHEBA ·

MARION KHALIDI

· AKBAR ·

JULIA MARSHALL

· CHENG HO ·

JULIA MARSHALL

· ALEXANDER ·

DENYS JOHNSON-DAVIES

· AVICENNA ·

REZA SHAH-KAZEMI

· RUMI ·

DENYS JOHNSON-DAVIES

EXHIBITION COLLECTION